HAL•LEONARD
INSTRUMENTAL
PLAY-ALONG

AUDIO
ACCESS
INCLUDED

PLAYBACK+
Speed • Pitch • Balance • Loop

T0061498

TRUMPET

THE GREATEST SHOWMAN

Audio Arrangements by Peter Deneff

To access audio visit:
www.halleonard.com/mylibrary

Enter Code
4455-0024-4022-0586

ISBN 978-1-5400-2844-0

HAL•LEONARD®
7777 W. BLUEMOUND RD. P.O. BOX 13819 MILWAUKEE, WI 53213

In Australia Contact:
Hal Leonard Australia Pty. Ltd.
4 Lentara Court
Cheltenham, Victoria, 3192 Australia
Email: ausadmin@halleonard.com.au

Visit Hal Leonard Online at
www.halleonard.com

COME ALIVE

TRUMPET

Words and Music by BENJ PASEK
and JUSTIN PAUL

FROM NOW ON

TRUMPET

Words and Music by BENJ PASEK
and JUSTIN PAUL

THE GREATEST SHOW

TRUMPET

Words and Music by BENJ PASEK,
JUSTIN PAUL and RYAN LEWIS

A MILLION DREAMS

TRUMPET

Words and Music by BENJ PASEK
and JUSTIN PAUL

NEVER ENOUGH

TRUMPET

Words and Music by BENJ PASEK
and JUSTIN PAUL

THE OTHER SIDE

TRUMPET

Words and Music by BENJ PASEK
and JUSTIN PAUL

REWRITE THE STARS

TRUMPET

Words and Music by BENJ PASEK
and JUSTIN PAUL

THIS IS ME

TRUMPET

Words and Music by BENJ PASEK
and JUSTIN PAUL

TIGHTROPE

TRUMPET

Words and Music by BENJ PASEK
and JUSTIN PAUL